LETTERS to a SOLDIER

America America America America Am...

Dear David,

You're very brave! It...
It also must be very...
name is Eric and I a...
was in a war too. I t...
the South Korean...
I also like to play...
Jets. My favorite food is mac...
people like you who save ou...

From,
Eric

God Bless America

By First Lieutenant David Falvey and Mrs. Julie Hutt's Fourth-Grade Class

two lions

two lions

Amazon Publishing
Attn: Amazon Children's Publishing
P.O. Box 400818
Las Vegas, NV 89140
www.amazon.com/amazonchildrenspublishing

Library of Congress Cataloging-in-Publication Data

Falvey, David (David A.)
  Letters to a soldier / by 1st Lt. David Falvey and Mrs. Julie Hutt's fourth-grade class.
    p. cm.
  ISBN 978-1-4778-4795-4
1. Iraq War, 2003—Personal narratives, American. 2. Falvey, David (David A.)—Correspondence. 3. Soldiers—United States—Correspondence. 4. Children's writings, American—New York (State) I. Title.
  DS79.76.F355 2009
  956.7044'33092—dc22

My love and thanks go to my family—my husband, Jon, and our three beautiful children, Jennifer, Laura, and Eric—for their never-ending support.

Last but not least, I'd like to thank the women and men who selflessly serve our country. They are the true heroes who preserve the freedom we enjoy. I am happy that three percent of the proceeds from this book will be donated to Fisher House™ Foundation, Inc., which supports America's military in their time of need.

—Julie Hutt

2008050268
Publisher's note: The letters and emails included in this book have been designed and edited only for clarity and to remove repetitions. The opinions and attitudes expressed in these letters and emails reflect individual beliefs and should not be taken to reflect the opinions and attitudes of the United States Military or the Roslyn, New York, school district. Thank you to Mrs. Julie Hutt and the students whose letters and artwork made this book possible. The artwork was created by: Kyler (jacket front), Ryan (jacket back), Katie and Brittney (title page, top and bottom), Sanaria (copyright page), Kyle (with Sanaria's letter), Alex (with Jason's letter), Sarah (with Carly's letter), Krystina (with Brittney's letter), Renny (with Evan's letter), Dorit (with Sam's letter), Eric (with his letter), Michelle (with Nick's letter), Mollie (with Katie's letter), Maddy (with her letter), Ciara (with Ryan's letter), and Fiona (with Kevin's letter). Thanks also to Mrs. Julie Hutt for the photographs on the last page.

Book design by Virginia Pope
Editor: Robin Benjamin

This book is dedicated to the memory of
the bravest person I've ever known,
Sergeant Scott A. Miller of 2nd platoon,
972nd Military Police Company.

—D.F.

December 9, 2008

The war in Iraq began during my junior year of college in March of 2003, while I was learning to be an Army officer through the University of Massachusetts' Army Reserve Officers Training Corps (ROTC) program. President George W. Bush said there were three reasons for going to war against Iraq: to disarm the country of weapons of mass destruction, to end Saddam Hussein's support of terrorism, and to free the Iraqi people. Iraq, led by President Saddam Hussein, was said to possess stockpiles of weapons of mass destruction. Many countries, such as the United States, felt threatened at the thought of a dangerous world leader having such powerful weapons. Weapons inspectors from the United Nations were sent to Iraq in November of 2002, with little result. That December, Saddam Hussein issued a declaration to the UN denying that Iraq had any weapons of mass destruction. The US claimed the declaration was untruthful, and the UN stated it was incomplete. On March 7, 2003, the US, along with allies Spain and Great Britain, ordered that Saddam Hussein give up all banned weapons by March 17, 2003, or face military action. Three days after this deadline passed, the war in Iraq began.

Rocket attack in Baghdad that began on Easter, 2008

I knew it was only a matter of time before I ended up going to war in either Iraq or Afghanistan, where we'd been fighting terrorist threats since 2001. In May of 2004, I graduated from the University of Massachusetts at Amherst and was promoted to the rank of 2nd Lieutenant in the Massachusetts Army National Guard. My first assignment was to serve as a platoon leader in the 972nd Military Police Company out of Reading, MA. As a platoon leader, I was responsible for leading forty-two Soldiers, which is no small task for a twenty-two-year-old. By the summer of 2006, we knew that in one year we would be deploying to Iraq. In October of 2007, after months of training and preparation, the 171 Soldiers of the 972nd Military Police Company reached Iraq to begin a nine month tour of duty in Baghdad, Iraq's capital. (Our arrival in Baghdad happened to be in the same month that our beloved Boston Red Sox won their second World Series title in four years.) At the time our company arrived, the number of US troops in Iraq was around 162,000.

Our mission was to conduct a security detail for the seven highest ranking government officials in Iraq: Prime Minister Nouri al-Maliki, President Jalal Talabani,

Vice President Tariq al-Hashimi, Vice President Adil Abdul-Mahdi, Speaker of the Council of Representatives Mahmoud al-Mashhadani, former Prime Minister Ayad Allawi, and former Prime Minister Ibrahim al-Jaafari. We also provided security details for high ranking officials visiting from other countries, such as US Vice President Dick Cheney and French Foreign Minister Bernard Kouchner. Terrorists often target high ranking government officials for attack because injuring or killing these officials makes the country they serve look weak and unstable, which is what the terrorists want. It was our responsibility to escort these officials throughout Baghdad to ensure their safety during their entire visit.

Being 6,000 miles away in Iraq, I wanted to make sure my friends and family back home heard from me frequently. I wanted them to know I was okay, and I also wanted them to know what life in Iraq was like for me. I was lucky to have so much support, and I usually received packages and letters daily. During my tour, I received an envelope filled with personalized letters and drawings from Mrs. Hutt's fourth-grade class in Long Island, New York. Receiving the letters was important for me because it allowed me to briefly forget the serious nature of my life in Baghdad. I received fun questions about my favorite sports team or if I had a dog back home. I also received clever questions about what I was doing in Iraq and what life was like here. It was clear that these students simply wanted to hear from me, and I was excited about sharing my experiences with them. Coming up with my responses to the letters was challenging and revealing. Some of the questions were very difficult to answer, and I wanted to be careful in my responses. One of the questions I received was "Why are we fighting for Iraq's freedom?" This is not an easy question for anyone to answer. But I did the best I could to share my experiences with Mrs. Hutt's class, and my hope is that they benefited from my responses even a little bit. I certainly did.

The 972nd Military Police Company arrived back in the US on June 27, 2008 (ten days after the Boston Celtics won their seventeenth NBA Championship). After spending nine months in Iraq, we were fortunate to come home with all of our Soldiers. I have since returned to a reserve status with the Massachusetts Army National Guard, and I'm currently working as a civilian contractor for the US Air Force at Hanscom Air Force Base. Though I've been back for five months, I will never forget my tour of duty in Iraq.

David Falvey

Mission ready!

January 18, 2008

Dear David,

    Hi! We have met a few times over the years. I teach fourth grade here in New York, and my students decided that they would like to write to someone serving in the military. I thought about you and asked for your address. Needless to say, my students were very excited to hear about you and to write to you. I told them I knew you, and they had so many questions. Most of my students are nine, turning ten, so what they write is reflective of their age. Their letters are enclosed.

    I hope you are doing well and staying safe. All the best to you and the others who serve along with you. Thank you for all that you do.

Fondly,

Julie Hutt

P.S. I have also shared the pictures that you sent with my students. I wish you could have seen their reactions! You are a hero!! ☺

April 29, 2008

Hi Julie, it's David Falvey. I'm sorry it took so long to get back to you and your students. I've been pulling double duty as Executive Officer (XO) since our XO went on leave. I have been very busy. I really appreciate the letters I got from your students. I can't tell you how much easier it is for us knowing how much support we have back home, and letters like these prove that to us. I personally answered each question. I apologize if some of the responses are a little long, but there were some tough questions that were asked. I hope some of these answers weren't too above their heads; as I'm sure you know, the situation over here is complex, and it can be tough to understand for a 40-year-old, let alone a fourth grader.

Hi class, my name is David Falvey. I'm a 25-year-old from Billerica, Massachusetts, but I've lived in Boston for the last few years. I'm currently serving in Baghdad, Iraq, with my Army National Guard unit out of Reading, Massachusetts, the 972nd Military Police Company. I was grateful to receive your letters, and you asked some pretty great questions, which I'm answering all by email now.

The acting XO in his office—
notice the mustache

Blue Blue Blue!!!

I
i
k
e

t
h
e

o
u
t
d
o
o
r
s

Dear David,

It must be hard in the army. What do you do there? Let me introduce myself. My name is Sanaria and I'm 9 years old. I like to read, draw, and play computer. I have an annoying little brother and my favorite color is blue and orange. I also play the flute. I like to play volleyball, ping pong, and etc. Tell me about yourself.

(I am Korean)

Your friend,

Sanaria

I HOPE this puts a ☺ on ur face!

I
L
U
V

A
N
I
M
A
L
S
!
!
!

Sanaria—

What do you do in the Army? Everyone in the military has a specific job. Some people are mechanics or cooks. Others are pilots or doctors or infantry soldiers. My job is a Military Police (MP) officer, and it is a job with many different functions. We may be in charge of enemy prisoners, convoy security—where we make sure vehicles holding key personnel or cargo make it to the desired location—law and order missions, police intelligence missions, reconnaissance, and missions where we train the Iraqis how to serve as police officers themselves. In my case, we do a lot of convoy security.

We collaborated with the Air Force to deliver clothes, toys, food, books, and office supplies to a school in Baghdad. We were greeted by children eager to get their hands on whatever they could, and afterward, we all played soccer in the schoolyard.

Dear David,

Hello my name is Jason. I want
to thank you for being so brave.
I wish the war was over so you
can come home. I am worrying
about you. What do you do in Iraq?
Do you take breaks? How long have
you been in Iraq? You must be
a strong man. Please come home
safely. I will be thinking
about you.

Love,
Jason

Jason—

What do I do in the war? I have many different jobs over here, but I have one main job. I am a platoon leader, and my job is to lead a platoon of 42 Soldiers. If you have seen the movie *Forrest Gump*, Lieutenant Dan is Forrest's platoon leader. I am in the same position as Lieutenant Dan! I am completely in charge of these 42 Soldiers, and it is my job to look out for every aspect of their lives here. I am responsible for everything that has to do with them, and if our platoon has a mission, it is my job to lead my 42 Soldiers to complete that mission successfully. It is a lot of responsibility, but I have 42 GREAT Soldiers and it's a great job to serve with them.

How long have I been in Iraq? I have been in Iraq now for 7 months, and I have two months left.

Many Soldiers stop in Kuwait before they head north to Iraq. In our case, it gave us an opportunity to get used to the time difference, weather, and terrain. We were there for two weeks, and this was our tent—we were a bit cramped.

Dear David,

My name is Carly. I hope you're okay. I do wonder what it is like to be a soldier and what you would do in your spare time? How is Iraq different from America? Wow, it must be hard work being a soldier!

Sincerely,

Carly

P.S. Good Luck and Stay Safe!

Iraq has many mosques, where Muslims worship. From the minaret, or tower, you will hear a "call to prayer" five times a day. It sounds like a man singing in Arabic and is very majestic. Calls to prayer can be very loud, and you can often hear several calls throughout the city because of the many mosques.

Carly—

What's it like being a Soldier? It's not an easy thing to be. There are a lot of sacrifices, such as working very long hours and having to go to dangerous places like Iraq. But it is also a tremendous experience. You become very close with your fellow Soldiers, and the selflessness and diligence you must possess will carry over into the rest of your life. The work we do is challenging, meaningful, and fulfilling. You feel like you're part of something big and important. A decision made by a 17- or 18-year-old Soldier in Iraq or Afghanistan may have a tremendous effect on the world. You never forget that.

What do we do in our spare time? Our spare time isn't much different from yours. We are lucky enough to be on a base that has electricity and satellites, so we do get some TV, and Soldiers can play video games and use the Internet. We have a library with plenty of books. Some days we are very busy and have little time for these things, and some days are less busy. It depends on each Soldier's specific job. I, for one, never seem to have spare time!!

How is Iraq different from America? Iraq is very different from the US but, as in every society, we are all people, and the average American and average Iraqi aren't as different as you might think. The weather is very hot, and there are a lot of palm trees and sand. Many houses include not just a mother and father with their children but also aunts, uncles, cousins, and grandparents, and often they all sleep in the same common room. Women usually wear traditional dress that covers most of their body. Iraq is a very divided country, and that is much of the reason it is so dangerous. The Muslim religion is split into Sunnis and Shi'as, and both are in Baghdad and throughout Iraq, and they don't get along well. There is also an ethnic group called the Kurds, and there are Christians. These groups all fight for power and influence. In the US, most people come from different ethnic and religious backgrounds, and that is celebrated or not looked at as a big deal. In Iraq, these differences are a big deal.

Dear David,

I think that it's a very nice thing that you are doing. Last night I was confused. Why are we fighting for Iraq's freedom? Do some people not want freedom? My great grandpa Henry was in the war. So whenever I think of him I think of you! I love dogs. My aunt has 3. My favorite things to do are jump on my bed, watch T.V., and go on the computer!

From,
Brittney

Brittney—

Why are we fighting for Iraq's freedom. Do some people not want freedom? Great question, and I wish the answer was easy. We are fighting for Iraq's freedom because the Middle East, where Iraq and Afghanistan are located, is an area of the world that is home to various terrorist groups, such as Al-Qaeda, that want to do bad things to the US and its allies. The hope with Iraq is to have a free country in the heart of the Middle East, where Al-Qaeda is unwelcome, and that this freedom will spread throughout the Middle East, creating a safer world. Iraq is now a government that is elected by the people and is representative of the people, and the people have the ability to listen to whatever music they want, watch whatever movies they want, read any newspaper they want. It was not like this before.

Terrorist groups like Al-Qaeda want everyone to convert to their religion and lead extremely strict lives, and the government would control people to make sure these strict rules are followed. This is what Afghanistan was like before 2001 with the Taliban in power. Groups like Al-Qaeda hate the US because the US allows its free citizens to watch MTV and listen to whatever music they want and read whatever book or newspaper they want. Al-Qaeda feels this freedom is a threat to their ability to control people, and this is why they do not like countries like the US. It's a clash of civilizations.

This is one of the most prominent mosques, the Abu Hanifah Mosque in Baghdad's Adhamiyah neighborhood. Our unit traveled there to allow the prime minister of Iraq to safely pay a visit.

Dear David,

Hi, my name is Evan. I am soo happy you are serving our country. How many years have you been in the army? When is the war going to be over? I lost my tooth yesterday. Are you the leader? My grandpa was in the army. I think he served in World War 2. Are you a Boston Red Sox fan? My teacher told me you are from Boston. I am a huge Boston fan! I go every year and I am from New York. Hope you come home soon. Good Luck!

Your New Friend,
Evan

Evan—

How long have I been in the Army? Six years next month, and my current rank is 1st Lieutenant.

When is the war going to be over? The President of the United States is our Commander-in-Chief, and it is his decision. The goal is to leave Iraq when Iraq has the ability to keep itself secure from foreign threats and threats from terrorist groups and militia groups within Iraq. At this time, Iraq is not at that point but hopefully will be soon.

Am I a Red Sox fan? I am a HUUUGE Red Sox fan, and I also spend a lot of time rooting against the Yankees. I watched the Red Sox win the World Series here in Baghdad back in October. Evan, I admire your bravery in being a Sox fan in the heart of New York. You are clearly a very smart young man.

Iraq doesn't have the same standards for electricity, construction, and plumbing as in the US. Buildings often look like they're falling apart and covered in wires. The pipes are so narrow that you can't flush toilet paper. You put it in the trash. I never got used to that! Hopefully as Iraq becomes stable, it can spend money on construction projects to fix these problems.

Dear David,

I have heard you are serving our country. We appreciate you so so much. I have a dog named Reily. My name is Sam. I love the Yankees. I also have two cats. Their names are Sparkles and Molly. Well, that's all.

From,
Sam

Sam—

I see you're a big Yankees fan. . . . We are going to have some problems!! No, just kidding. My college roommate is a huge Yankees fan, and somehow he manages to be one of my best friends. Baseball would be nothing without the Yankees and the Red Sox!!

We don't have a field to play baseball, but we do have a basketball court we use often . . . except in sandstorms!

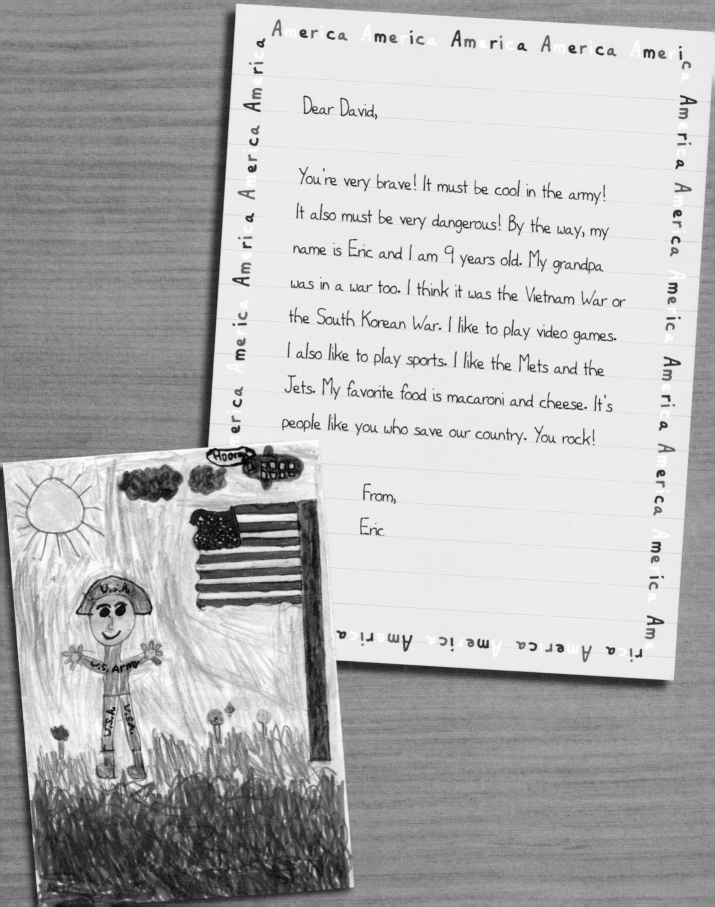

America America America America America

Dear David,

You're very brave! It must be cool in the army!
It also must be very dangerous! By the way, my
name is Eric and I am 9 years old. My grandpa
was in a war too. I think it was the Vietnam War or
the South Korean War. I like to play video games.
I also like to play sports. I like the Mets and the
Jets. My favorite food is macaroni and cheese. It's
people like you who save our country. You rock!

From,
Eric

Eric—

You're right, it IS cool being in the Army. I'm enjoying every minute of it, though I am excited about returning home to see my friends and family.

The Christmas spirit is alive even in Baghdad— my door on Christmas Eve

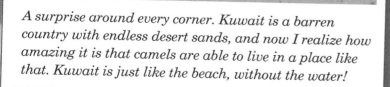

A surprise around every corner. Kuwait is a barren country with endless desert sands, and now I realize how amazing it is that camels are able to live in a place like that. Kuwait is just like the beach, without the water!

Dear David,

I'm Nick. My favorite things to do are play outside and read. What are your favorite things to do? Has your mom, dad, grandpa or grandma ever been in a war? My favorite color is blue and red. What's your favorite color? My favorite book is Harry Potter. What's your favorite book? Hope you come home before school ends!

From,

Nick

Nick—

What are my favorite things to do? I like to travel a lot. When you're in the Army and you have to go to Iraq, the Army gives you 15 days of vacation and they will fly you anywhere in the world for free. Most people go home, but I decided to go to Australia. It was great! I like sports a lot and I've been trying to keep up, but because we are 7 hours ahead of you, most games are on at 3 in the morning.

Has anyone in my family ever been to war? There aren't many people in my family that have been to war. My uncle was in Vietnam, and my brother-in-law was a sailor in the Persian Gulf War. Most of the other people in my family either chose not to go into the service or were disqualified due to medical reasons.

My favorite color? I have a favorite color for each different object. I like my car silver, my jeans blue, my grass green, and my shirts usually white. I know, I'm crazy.

My favorite book? I have two. . . . One is *Black Hawk Down*, which was turned into a movie. It's a tremendous story written about a battle that occurred in 1993 in Somalia between the United States military and Somalian militants. The story is from both the Somalian and American sides, so it is a great way to understand both sides of how the battle went down. In the military, this book is very famous because it does such a great job of teaching us what we did wrong in the battle and how to do it better next time. The other is *All Souls*, which is a book about growing up in a famous part of Boston called South Boston and the struggles this one boy had, along with his several siblings. It's a great Boston story, and I love Boston!

A mission from Baghdad to Balad Air Base, just to the north, via Black Hawk helicopter

Our wingman and the view

Dear David,

Peace

My name is Katie. I have a dog. My dog's name is Cooper. My dog even has a middle name. My dog's middle name is Prince. Do you have any pets? I think my grandfather was in the Marines. Good Luck!

Sincerely,
Katie

Smile
Smile
Smile

My dog Brady back home

Katie—

Do I have any pets? I do have a dog, and his name is Brady. He is half mini-pinscher, half dachshund. I miss him very, very much. We see one family of wild dogs in a neighborhood in Baghdad we go to often. They live on their own and are a little more rough than dogs back in the US. Most Iraqis do not keep dogs as pets, as it is not considered clean. I think most people ignore these dogs. They love seeing American Soldiers because of how much we love playing with them and petting them, and it reminds us of our dogs.

They're cute even when they're picking through trash.

Dear David,

Let me introduce myself. Hi, my name is
Maddy. I have a dog named Mugzy. When
I grow up, I want to be an animal
police person. Do you like animals? I play
the guitar and the trumpet. Do you play
any musical instruments? My grandpa
was in the Russian war. Don't worry.
He was with the American army and is
still alive. I hope you could come and see
us in school one day.

Your 4th grade pen pal,
Maddy

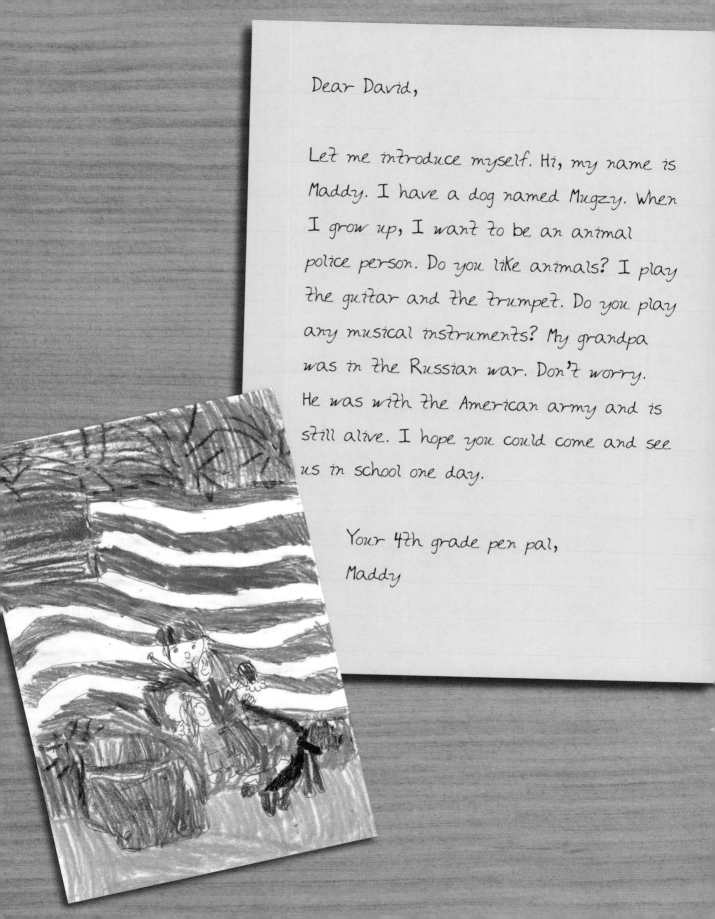

Maddy—

Do I like animals? I do like animals. I don't get to see too many here besides the dogs I mentioned. We have a company cat we see and feed often, named Caramel. She is a very sweet cat. I see a lot of lizards around here, but that is about it. I actually miss seeing squirrels, if you can believe that!

Do I play any instruments? I don't play any instruments, though I sing a lot! I used to spend my time singing in the car and I can't do that here, so I'll sing in my room. Soldiers that live near me laugh at that, but I have to do it! I want to learn to play the piano when I get back. I should have started when I was your age because if I had, I'd be a pro by now. So take my advice: keep up with the trumpet and guitar!!

Caramel, our mascot—don't let the eyes
fool you, he's the friendliest cat

To David,

Hello. My name is Ryan. I'm
sure you have saved 1,000
lives already. Keep protecting.
One day, I think I might join the
military. For Halloween 2 years
ago, I was a soldier dude. I
like sushi. My dad was born
in Iran. My friend is Eric. He
wrote to you too. I like reading
comic books and video games.

Your new friend,
Ryan

Ryan—

I am glad to hear that you're interested in joining the military. Fortunately, you have many years until you have to make that important decision. It is a great thing that we have a volunteer military so people can decide for themselves if they want to serve. Being a Soldier is a great job. . . . It is also a tremendous sacrifice. Think long and hard to make sure it's a sacrifice that you want to make.

The end of the day in Kuwait

Dear David,

I'm glad you're serving our country.
How is Iraq? I worry about you. How
are you doing? I hope you are feeling
good. About me, I'm in 4th grade. My
name is Kevin. I have lots of friends.
Please be careful.

Sincerely,
Kevin

Kevin—

You sound so genuine in your letter when you say you worry about me and to please be careful. I promise you I will make it back safely, and I am grateful to have fine Americans like yourself looking out for me.

Thank you all for your letters! You are all fine Americans.

David Falvey
First Lieutenant, Military Police

"Welcome Home Ceremony" for our unit at the historic Faneuil Hall in Boston, with Senator John Kerry as the keynote speaker

Mrs. Hutt and her teaching assistant, Lauren Sarokoff

Mrs. Hutt's fourth-grade class

Two students who were absent in the original photo

When asked as a child, "What do you want to be when you grow up?" I would answer, "A teacher." I also knew I wanted to be a mom. Today, I am fortunate to be both.

My philosophy of life is pretty basic—caring for others and giving back to the world. This prompted me to ask my students to write to a Soldier, First Lieutenant Dave Falvey of the United States Army, who my relatives knew was stationed in Iraq. My class's enthusiasm was genuine and sparked a wealth of questions from the curious minds of nine- and ten-year olds. We had fabulous discussions about heroes, and about helping and caring for those we might never know or meet. The atmosphere of warmth and sincerity was infectious!

I never imagined that my students' letters and artwork would lead to the publication of a book. My thanks go to Robin Benjamin, whose vision for this project has now come to fruition, and Dave Falvey, not only for his service to his country, but for taking the time to answer each letter and to acknowledge the children's wonderful artwork. I also want to thank and compliment all of my students for their efforts and unconditional compassion toward others. I am very proud of each and every one of them.

—Julie Hutt

Would you like to write letters to a soldier?

Besides writing to a soldier you know, you could ask your teacher, parent, or guardian to look at organizations such as www.mysoldier.com for programs that connect you or your class with a soldier pen pal.

34062560R00020

Made in the USA
Charleston, SC
28 September 2014